D0131072

HAVE YOU EVER SEEN

a SMACK of
JELLYFISH?

AN ALPHABET BOOK

SARAH ASPER-SMITH

SASQUATCH BOOKS
SEATTLE

This one's for the boys:
Pat, Aaron, and Lou

HAVE YOU EVER SEEN...

an ARMY of ANTS?

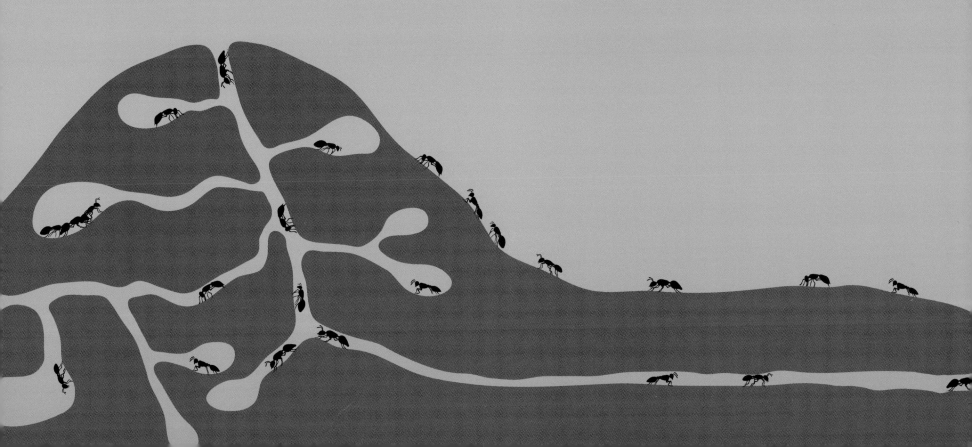

a FLUTTER of
BUTTERFLIES?

a MURDER of CROWS?

a TEAM
of DUCKS?

a PARADE of ELEPHANTS?

a KNOT of FROGS?

a GAGGLE of GEESE?

a BLOAT of HIPPOPOTAMUSES?

a MESS of IGUANAS?

a TROOP of KANGAROOS?

a PRIDE of LIONS?

a SCOURGE of
MOSQUITOES?

a WATCH of NIGHTINGALES?

a PARLIAMENT of OWLS?

a STRING of PONIES?

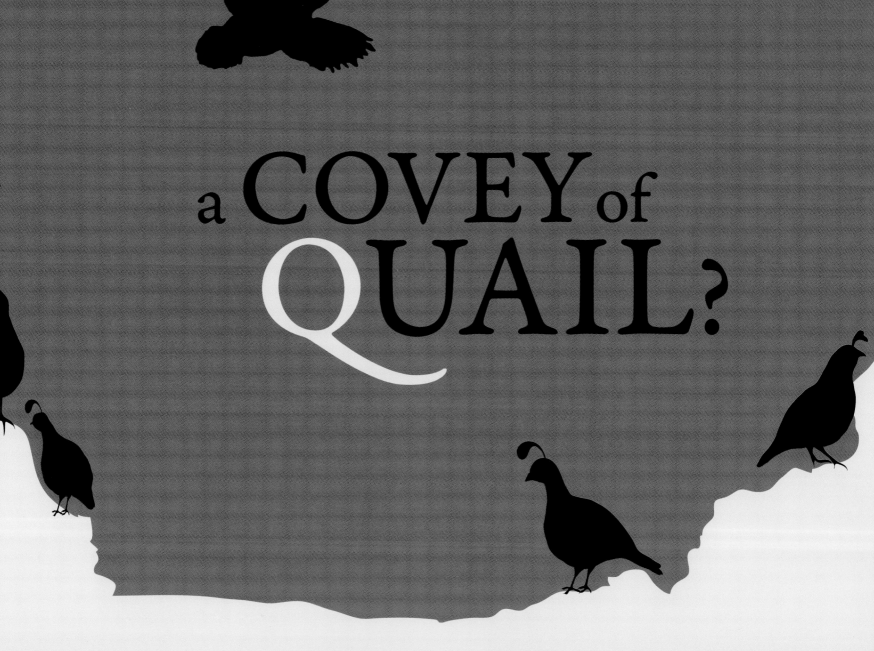

a COVEY of
QUAIL?

a CRASH of RHINOCEROSES?

a WALK of SNAILS?

a BALE of TURTLES?

a BED of URCHINS?

a POD of WHALES?

a SCHOOL of X-RAY FISH?

a HERD of YAKS?

a ZEAL of ZEBRAS?

Manufactured in China in October 2010 by C&C Offset Printing Co. Ltd. Shenzhen, Guangdong Province
Published by Sasquatch Books
Distributed by PGW/Perseus
15 14 13 12 11 10   9 8 7 6 5 4 3 2 1

Cover and interior illustration/design: Sarah Asper-Smith
Cover and interior composition: Kate Basart/Union Pageworks

Library of Congress Cataloging-in-Publication Data is available.
ISBN-13: 978-1-57061-687-7
ISBN-10: 1-57061-687-6

SASQUATCH BOOKS
119 South Main Street, Suite 400
Seattle, WA 98104
206/467-4300
www.sasquatchbooks.com | custserv@sasquatchbooks.com